CLOTH LULLABY

THE WOVEN LIFE OF LOUISE BOURGEOIS

WORDS BY
AMY NOVESKY

PICTURES BY
ISABELLE ARSENAULT

ABRAMS BOOKS FOR YOUNG READERS

NEW YORK

LOUISE WAS RAISED BY A RIVER.

HER FAMILY LIVED IN A BIG HOUSE ON THE WATER
THAT WOVE LIKE A WOOL THREAD THROUGH EVERYTHING.

THE RIVER'S SOIL NURTURED A GARDEN
WHERE LOUISE AND HER FAMILY GREW
GERANIUMS, PEONIES, ASPARAGUS, AND
CHERRY TREES; APPLES AND PEARS,
PURPLE TAMARISK, PINK HAWTHORN, AND
SWEET-SMELLING HONEYSUCKLE.

ALONG ITS BANKS,
HER FATHER PLANTED POPLARS.

LOUISE KEPT DIARIES OF HER
DAYS. AND IN A CLOTH TENT
PITCHED IN THE GARDEN,
SHE AND HER SIBLINGS WOULD STAY
TILL THE DARK SURPRISED THEM,
THE LIGHT FROM THE HOUSE,
AND THE SOUND OF A VERDI OPERA,
FAR AWAY THROUGH THE TREES.

SOMETIMES, THEY'D SPEND THE NIGHT,
AND LOUISE WOULD STUDY THE
WEB OF STARS, IMAGINE HER PLACE
IN THE UNIVERSE, AND WEEP,
THEN FALL ASLEEP TO THE RHYTHMIC
ROCK AND MURMUR OF RIVER WATER.

THE RIVER PROVIDED FLOWERS AND FRUIT,
A LULLABY, AND A LIVELIHOOD.

LOUISE'S FAMILY RESTORED TAPESTRIES
— ART WOVEN FROM WOOL — AND THE WOOL
LOVED THE TANNIN-RICH WATERS,
WHICH CLEANSED AND STRENGTHENED IT,
AND ALLOWED IT TO SOAK UP COLOR.

At the family's workshop, Louise's mother, like her mother before her, repaired fabric grown threadbare with time.

She loved to work in the warm sun, her needle rising and falling beside the lilting river, perfect, delicate spiderwebs glinting with caught drops of water above her.

AND WHEN LOUISE
WAS TWELVE YEARS OLD,
SHE LEARNED THE TRADE, TOO,
DRAWING IN THE MISSING
FRAGMENTS OF A TAPESTRY.

IT WAS OFTEN THE BOTTOMS OF THESE FABRIC PICTURES
THAT GOT THE MOST WEAR
AND WERE MOST IN NEED OF REPAIR,
AND SO LOUISE BECAME ADEPT AT DRAWING FEET.
DRAWING WAS *LIKE A THREAD IN A SPIDER'S WEB.*

AMONG TAPESTRIES NEATLY STACKED LIKE BOOKS IN A LIBRARY,
LOUISE'S MOTHER TAUGHT HER DAUGHTER ABOUT FORM AND
COLOR AND THE VARIOUS STYLES OF TEXTILES.
SOME BORE ELABORATE PATTERNS; OTHERS TOLD STORIES.

SHE TAUGHT HER ABOUT THE WARP AND THE WEFT, AND HOW TO WEAVE. THE TOOLS OF THEIR TRADE:

SPIRAL-SHAPED SPINDLES,

SPOOLS OF WOOL,

AND A NEEDLE.

SHE TAUGHT HER HOW TO DYE —
PURPLISH-RED WAS MADE FROM
CRUSHED COCHINEAL BUGS; INDIGO AND GAUDE,
OR YELLOW, FROM PLANTS;
BLACK WOOL CAME STRAIGHT
FROM THE BACKS OF BLACK
SHEEP —

AND THAT WOOL
SMELLED; THAT'S
HOW YOU KNEW
IT WAS REAL.

LOUISE'S MOTHER WAS HER BEST FRIEND.
DELIBERATE... PATIENT, SOOTHING...
SUBTLE, INDISPENSABLE... AND AS USEFUL
AS AN ARAIGNÉE (SPIDER).

LOUISE'S FATHER WAS NOT A RESTORER,
BUT HE APPRECIATED FINE THINGS.
HE BOUGHT LOUISE BEAUTIFUL
CLOTHES FROM PARISIAN
DEPARTMENT STORES.

BUT HE WAS ALWAYS LEAVING,
WHICH MADE LOUISE SO MAD,
SHE THREW HERSELF
INTO THE RIVER.

HE BROUGHT BACK CLOTH SCRAPS
FROM HIS TRAVELS, AND
LOUISE'S MOTHER FIXED THEM.

TWO HALVES OF A CLOTH
WOULD FIND THEIR WAY
BACK TOGETHER AGAIN.

RENTRAYAGE —
TO REWEAVE ACROSS THE CUT.

TO MAKE WHOLE.

LOUISE FOLLOWED THE RIVER TO PARIS,
WHERE IT FLOWED INTO THE SEINE.
LITTLE DID SHE KNOW THAT ONE DAY SOON
HER BELOVED RIVER WOULD BE GONE,
FILLED IN, FLOWING NO LONGER WITH
THE WATERS THE WOOL LOVED, BUT
WITH CARS ON THEIR WAY TO THE CITY,

A MEMORY.

AT THE UNIVERSITY, SHE STUDIED MATHEMATICS. SHE LIKED SUBJECTS
WITH STABILITY AND ORDER, LIKE GEOMETRY AND COSMOGRAPHY.
STARS WERE PREDICTABLE. SO, TOO, THE SUNRISE, THE SETTING OF THE
MOON. BUT SHE WAS DEEPLY DISAPPOINTED TO LEARN THAT MATH,
LIKE LIFE, IS UNCERTAIN.

WHILE SHE WAS STILL A STUDENT, HER MOTHER DIED. LOUISE WAS HEARTBROKEN. SHE FELT ABANDONED AND ALL ALONE.
A THREAD, BROKEN.

SHE ABANDONED MATH AND THE STARS AND TURNED TO PAINTING, APPLYING THE LESSONS SHE'D LEARNED SO FAR TO ART.

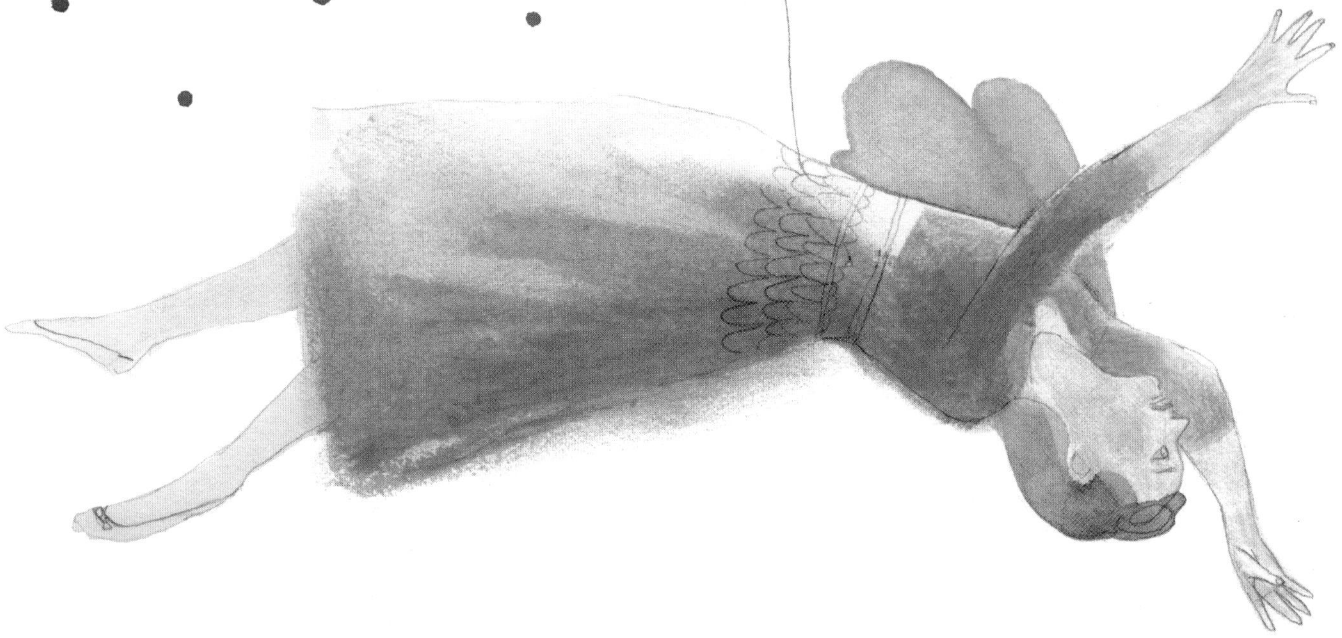

THE COLOR *BLUE*
PINCHES MY HEART.

SHE DREW,
SHE PAINTED,
SHE WOVE.
SHE MISSED HER MOTHER
SO MUCH, SHE SCULPTED
GIANT SPIDERS
MADE OF BRONZE, STEEL, AND MARBLE
SHE NAMED *MAMAN*.

HER MOTHER WAS NOT UNLIKE A SPIDER,
A REPAIRER OF BROKEN THINGS.

IF YOU BASH INTO THE WEB OF A SPIDER,
SHE DOESN'T GET MAD. SHE WEAVES AND SHE REPAIRS IT.

LOUISE GATHERED ALL THE FABRIC OF HER LIFE —

ALL THE DRESSES AND THE GARMENTS HER FATHER HAD BOUGHT HER; ALL THE BED LINENS, TOWELS, TABLECLOTHS, HER NEW HUSBAND'S HANDKERCHIEFS —

AND SHE CUT IT ALL UP.